Chasing After

faith

Mark E. Lingenfelter

Chasing After

*Capturing Hope
Through a Daughter's
Special Needs*

BMH Books
bmhbooks.com
P.O. Box 544
Winona Lake, IN 46590

Chasing After Faith
© 2012 by Mark E. Lingenfelter
ISBN:978-0-88469-280-5
RELIGION/ Christian Life/ Family

Scripture quotations marked NIV are taken from the Holy Bible, New International Version© NIV©. Copyright © 1973, 1978, 1984, by Biblica, Inc.™ Used by permission of Zondervan. All rights reserved worldwide. *www.zondervan.com*

Scripture quotations marked NASB are taken from the New American Standard Bible, © Copyright 1960, 1995 by the Lockman Foundation. Used by permission. (*www.lockman.org*)

Scripture quotations marked NLT are taken from the Holy Bible, New Living Translation, Copyright © 1996, 2004. Used by permission of Tyndale House Publishers, Inc., Wheaton, Illinois 60189. All rights reserved.

Scripture quotations marked MSG are taken from The Message. Copyright © 1993, 1994, 1995, 1996, 2000, 2001, 2002. Used by permission of NavPress Publishing Group.

The author has added italics to Scripture and quotations for emphasis.

Table of Contents

Acknowledgments

My daughter Faith.
For being perfect just the way you are and
providing me with plenty of sermon material.

My wife Angie for loving me and being an
amazing partner in life and ministry.

Kim, Janice, Jake, Cheryl and Michelle for helping
me with early content editing and advice.

Dan and Tom for going out on a limb and
endorsing my first book. Thanks for letting me
ride your coat tails.

Terry and the team at BMH books for giving me
this opportunity and providing amazing support
and guidance. You truly made this whole process
fun and rewarding.

Introduction

This book is NOT a record of woes and hardship. This book is NOT a pool of self-pity or sorrows. This is a book about the JOY found growing in the soil of suffering. It is intended to challenge the reader to consider the value of chasing after a life of faith.

I met a man who had a son born with a condition that will eventually result in the boy's becoming deaf. This has been a huge challenge to the man's faith. He questions God's love. He wonders why God would allow his child to suffer when so many evil people in the world seem to be untouched by such hardship. It is for this man and many like him that I wrote this book.

There have been, and will continue to be, many more difficult circumstances than our family has experienced with our daughter Faith. I have met men in Africa who have experienced severe persecution that I cannot begin to relate to. I have preached several funerals for families that have experienced the unimaginable pain of the death of a child. I do not pretend to know or understand the full measure of pain that others have experienced in this fallen world. However, I do know that those who have chosen to chase after a life of faith have avoided a lifetime of bitterness. They have experienced a supernatural peace and joy that transcend all understanding. My hope and prayer is that God will use the words in this book to encourage your heart, challenge your mind, and perhaps even change your life as you consider what it means to *Chase After Faith*.

Mark E. Lingenfelter, Roaring Spring, Pa.

How to Use this Book

This book can be used for personal reading, small group discussion, or one-on-one discipleship. If you are reading this book by yourself, you may still benefit from the discussion questions. The questions are designed to help the reader interact with God's Word and grow in his or her faith.

If you are using this book for a small group Bible study, the leader should distribute books to group members one week prior to the first group meeting. Instruct group members to read the first chapter so they will be prepared for the discussion questions. Encourage group members NOT to read ahead. Although the chapters are not long, the tension from week to week will keep members excited and engaged. At the end of each week's Bible study assign the following chapter and the "Chasing After Faith" section to be completed before the next meeting. The "Chasing After Faith" section at the end of each discussion is intended to be a personal and practical application of each chapter. It would be good to follow up with group members the following week on their experiences.

Since the purpose of this book is to encourage people to chase after a life of faith, consider asking someone who is struggling in their faith or going through a difficult circumstance to read a chapter a week with you and discuss it at a mutually agreed-upon time and place. The discussion questions could be a great way to open up dialogue in a discipleship setting.

Thank you for choosing this resource. My prayer is that God will use this book to bless many lives and draw people into a closer relationship with Him.

Pastor Mark E. Lingenfelter

Chapter 1

Her Name is Faith

"…I know the plans I have for you," declares the Lord, "plans to prosper
you and not to harm you, plans to give you hope and a future…"
Jeremiah 29:11 (NIV)

This may seem like an odd way to start a book, but I want you to say
your *NAME* out loud. Yes, the whole thing from start to finish. Let
it roll off your tongue like you were being introduced as the keynote
speaker of a conference or the prizefighter in the main event. If you
are reading this book in a public place (like the subway or the gym),
shouting your full name among random strangers should probably be
avoided.

Just think. Somewhere in the past your parent(s) said *your* name
out loud and decided *this* would be *your* name. Some of you really
like what you hear. The first name and the middle name seem to fit
together like a good peanut butter and jelly sandwich. Or perhaps you
cringe at the sound of it. Maybe the first and middle name clash like a
pair of green pants and a blue shirt. Maybe you like the fact that your
name is unique or that it is ordinary. Or maybe you wonder what in
the world your parents were thinking when they told the nurse to type
such a bizarre or mundane name on your birth certificate.

Selecting a child's name is a significant and daunting responsibil-
ity. There are so many things we cannot choose for our children: the
color of their eyes and hair, the shape of their nose, the size of their

ears....whether or not they will be born with abnormalities. These genetic gifts, over which we have no control, go with them throughout life, but their NAMES...their NAMES are the life-long gifts we do get to choose for them. So you may applaud or abhor the choice your parents made, but I think we all wonder at some point, *"How did my parents choose my name?"*

Maybe your parents used one of those books filled with names, combing through thousands of possibilities until they came to one that caught their ear. Maybe you are named after your father or some other relative. Perhaps your name was chosen in honor of some important historical figure or maybe you have one of those hippie names that makes no sense.

My name is Mark Edmund Charles Lingenfelter. My first name is just a biblical name that my parents liked and my middle names are a tribute to my grandfathers. It sounds somewhat regal when you say it out loud, but imagine trying to write this lengthy handle in the first grade. When Bill Smith was outside playing at recess because he finished his homework, I was still writing out my obnoxiously long name. My parents then continued the two-middle-name tradition with my sister, Michelle Elizabeth Lynn Lingenfelter. That's thirty-three glorious letters, longer than the alphabet...awesome!

When the time came to name my own children, I knew I could not do much about the length of Lingenfelter, but I could use some self-control and only give them ONE middle name. So my wife, Angie, and I agreed that our oldest daughter would be named Hannah Pearl. We both liked the biblical name Hannah, and her middle name is a tribute to my grandmother whom we both loved and greatly admired. When we found out our second child would be a boy we quickly agreed that Elijah was a great first name, but since no family names seemed to fit for a middle name we chose James (one of our favorite books in the Bible).

In both cases, Angie and I had little difficulty or disagreement over this monumental decision. But that was not the case when we found out that a third bundle of joy was on the way. I'm still not sure why we had so much trouble deciding on a name, but at one point we thought we might be that couple that waited until the child was born and the sarcastic nurse would have to come in and say, "Did ya'll choose a name yet, or should I just write Jane Doe on the birth certificate?" Fortunately it never came to that.

It was mid-August when we took our annual vacation to the beach. This trip to Ocean City, Maryland, had been a long-standing tradition in my family, and now I was continuing the tradition and making special memories with my own children in the sands near the Atlantic Ocean. Angie was six months pregnant at the time, so I imagine we looked like quite a frazzled pair as Angie waddled through the sand with a 1½-year-old and a four-year-old in hand while I was carrying all the "necessary" beach equipment strapped to my back.

One evening as we were strolling the boardwalk, popping in and out of the different shops, browsing through beach jewelry and silly junior high humor T-shirts, we decided we would buy the kids mugs with their names on them. So we began the search through what seemed like hundreds of brightly colored mugs to find the names "Hannah" and "Elijah" printed on the side. Much like choosing their names in the first place, finding mugs with their names on them was not that challenging. The moment of difficulty came when Angie's motherly instincts kicked in and she said, "Well, we can't leave HER out. She is at the beach too," as she pointed to her rounded, beachball belly. "No, I suppose not," I said with a twinge of guilt for not remembering to include our unborn child in this monumental purchase. And just like that our casual walk along the boardwalk had turned into some sort of "do or die" situation threatening to leave us stranded at the beach until we both agreed on a suitable name for our third child.

After several attempts at humor with names that would ensure harassment as a teenager, we got down to business. We each held up various mugs, and with hope in our voices said, "what do you think of…?" Every suggestion was shot down with a wrinkled nose or an unenthusiastic "that's not bad." But then it happened. Like a moment of clarity through the sea of mugs before us…Angie held up the mug that read, "FAITH." I was immediately attracted to the name and gave her my approving nod as if to say, "Now we are getting somewhere." Then Angie began her closing argument. With tear-swollen eyes she said, "This pregnancy wasn't part of our plan and has me more than a little scared. But I keep coming back to the verse from Jeremiah that says, '*I know the plans I have for you," declares the Lord, "plans to prosper you and not to harm you, plans to give you hope and a future…*' (Jeremiah 29:11, NIV) As I've been praying and taking my feelings of being overwhelmed to God, I feel like He keeps saying, 'Have FAITH that I know what is best for your life.' I think her name should be FAITH." Well, how could I argue with a sermon like that?

With a tender heart and a sheepish grin I said, "Honey, I love the name Faith, but are you sure? Once I buy these mugs there's no going back!" She smiled and said, "I'm sure." It was one of those special moments in life that you never forget and it wasn't over. Although we were in the cluttered souvenir shop to find mugs and shirts for our children, my wife was about to give me a gift that I will treasure for the rest of my life. Angie gently held my hand, looked in my eyes and softly said, "What do you think of Faith Elizabeth?" I began to cry. My tears then unleashed the floodgates holding back the tears in Angie's eyes. Why such emotion over the mention of a simple name? Elizabeth was my mom's middle name. My mom absolutely loved the beach; she is the reason the beach is part of our annual vacation tradition. And it was on this very same boardwalk that my mom struggled to endure a colostomy bag from the cancer that was killing her just to have one last vacation with her family before she died two months later. I really loved and admired my mom, so to offer Elizabeth as the middle name for baby Faith meant more to me than my wife will ever know.

There we stood in the loud, busy boardwalk shop with our two sleepy children and our three personalized mugs, crying like two gushing water fountains. Realizing we looked really out of place in this happy-go-lucky atmosphere we awkwardly kissed, wiped our faces and then in the absence of a proper tissue I wiped my nose on my son's shirt. It was a moment I will forever cherish and one that would set the tone for stormy seas that were coming over the horizon. Little did we know that the phrase "*Have FAITH that God knows what is best for your life*" would become more than a path to our daughter's name, but a guide on how to live life after she was born.

DISCUSSION QUESTIONS
Chapter 1

1. Do you know the story behind your name? Do you like your name? Would you like to change it? Why or why not?

   Did you know that the believer in Jesus Christ will receive a NEW NAME in Heaven? Read Revelation 2:17. What do you hope your new name will be?

   Read 2 Corinthians 5:17. Write it out:

   Lots of really smart Bible scholars cannot agree over what this image is supposed to represent. A proper study of this verse would render at least a dozen possible meanings of the image of the white stone with a new name written on it. However, for the sake of our discussion, let's assume that the "new name" represents our new character and new nature we receive through faith in Jesus Christ.

   _____

   _____

   _____

If your name right now reflected your character, what might your name be? (Circle one)

Courage	Coward	Grace	Bitter
Faith	Worry	Humble	Proud
Content	Discontent		

What does 2 Corinthians 5:17 have to say about who you are and who you are becoming in your relationship with Jesus Christ?

2. The name of Jesus is a powerful name! It is the Greek form of Joshua and it means "*The Lord is salvation*" (Matthew 1:21). Read the following verses containing the NAMES and titles of Jesus. Write out the name or title that you find in each verse.

1 John 2:1 _____

Revelation 1:8 _____

Hebrews 5:9 _____

John 6:32 _____

John 10:11 _____

Romans 11:26 _____

1 Timothy 2:5 _____

1 Timothy 6:15 _____

How do these names or titles for Jesus impact your everyday life?

3. In the Old Testament God identified himself to Moses as "I AM" (Exodus 3:14). Then in Exodus 6:3 God tells Moses His name is _____.

Read the following verses containing the NAMES and titles of God. Write out the name or title that you find in each verse.

Genesis 17:1 _____

Deuteronomy 33:27 _____

2 Samuel 22:2 _____

Exodus 15:2 _____

Genesis 22:14 _____

Judges 6:24 _____

What do these names or titles for God teach us about the character and nature of God?

4. What do the following verses teach us about the relationship between our name and the name of Jesus Christ?

   Acts 4:12
   Romans 10:13
   Revelation 20:15

5. If you have children, how did you make that final decision about your child's name? As Mark and Angie came to a conclusion on a name for their third child, a verse from Jeremiah gave them guidance and comfort.

   Read Jeremiah 29:11. Write it out: _____

   _____

   _____

   How does this verse give you confidence that God knows what is best for your life? Give an example.

   When have you felt overwhelmed in life? How did you respond? How does a biblical perspective of life help us during difficult days?

Chasing After Faith

THIS WEEK: Give yourself a NEW NAME. Identify one character trait or strength you would like God to grow in you. Write out this desired quality or strength as your "new name" on a nametag. For example: "Mark the Unselfish" or "Angie the strong in faith." Place the nametag somewhere you will see it this week. Every time you see the nametag, pray that God will transform this area of your life.

Chapter 2
Faith is Born

"Give your entire attention to what God is doing right now, and don't get worked up about what may or may not happen tomorrow. God will help you deal with whatever hard things come up when the time comes."
Matthew 6:34 (MSG)

The day had finally arrived! This was the day that every mom, in those last uncomfortable weeks, yearns for. This was the day we had been looking forward to for nine months. This was the day we would meet our daughter Faith for the first time.

We had made plans for this day. Having been down this road twice before, we had certain expectations on how the day would unfold. According to our plan, we would check into our small rural hospital. Angie would take her position on the Serta/Craftmatic-like bed while I was forced to sleep in an uncomfortably narrow chair during the 18 hours of so-called "labor" (I never saw her get out of bed once to dig a ditch or shingle a roof); finally, the rudimentary finger gauge of the doctor reaches 10 centimeters and the real show begins. The nurses turn the spotlights on, the doctor snaps his rubber gloves, and I lovingly sacrifice my hand as a squeezing ball while coaching Angie to breathe and push. Before you get too angry about my "labor" joke above, let me just say that my wife is a warrior! She gave birth to three children with nothing more than Tylenol for the pain. And believe me when I say that she WORKED hard for every push!

This was how we expected the day to go. But life doesn't always play out as we expect. There are days we get out of bed expecting life to run smoothly and our plans to fall in line, only to be frustrated by misplaced keys, irritated by obstacles standing between us and our plans, and overwhelmed by that unexpected phone call that puts a U-turn in our day. Of course there are those who roll out of bed in the morning expecting rain clouds and detours, but Angie and I tend to expect the best from day to day. We are not naive to the pitfalls and curveballs of life. We have experienced plenty of each. However, we do not live in constant fear of what might be around the corner. Jesus said, "*Therefore do not worry about tomorrow, for tomorrow will worry about itself. Each day has enough trouble of its own*" (Matthew 6:34, NIV). Well, this was about to become one of those days of trouble.

From the moment Faith was born we both knew something was not right. Her color was bluish-gray. Her cry was weak and muffled, like a whimpering kitten's. I began to study the faces of the professionals in the room, looking for clues to confirm my suspicion that something was wrong. Angie took a more direct approach and asked, "Is she all right?" The staff assured us our newborn baby was fine, but as they whisked her over to the incubator bed for further examination, we locked eyes and without saying a word we agreed our new daughter was not fine.

After Faith was weighed, measured and examined the doctor repeated his initial assessment: "Congratulations, you have a healthy baby girl." Our fears subsided, but were not completely quenched. Over the next 24 hours, things went according to plan. Family and friends came to visit. I handed out candy bars with Faith's length and weight printed on them as I made jokes about how I had done most of the work. We prepared to take our daughter home. As I pulled the car into the loading zone on that cold Friday in November, I was expecting to see Angie and Faith at the door, bundled up and waiting to go home. They were not. I parked and made my way back to the room I had left only moments before. As I walked through the doors to the birthing unit I saw my wife and mother-in-law waiting in the hallway with that universal look of impending bad news on their faces. I had seen this look before. It was the look my mom had on her face when she was about to tell me that my dad had a heart attack. It was the look my dad had on his face when he was about to tell me that my mom had cancer. Now tightened jaws and tear-filled eyes met me again at the other end of this hallway, and my heart sank. My mind immediately began to fill with worst-case scenarios.

As Angie sank her red, tear-swollen face into my neck, I held her tightly and asked with a forced calm tone, "What's happening? Is Faith all right?" Her quivering response was the last thing I expected. Apparently, as Angie was holding Faith in her lap, dressing her to go home, she noticed Faith was missing the roof of her mouth. Our child had a cleft palate and somehow the doctor and the nurses all missed it. It still blows my mind that we were minutes from leaving the hospital when this significant discovery was made by the "professional" eye of my wife. I could understand if an underdeveloped organ went unnoticed, but a simple finger sweep of the mouth is supposed to be standard procedure.

When the doctor came in to see us he was very apologetic. I suppose in that moment we could have been very angry, but our emotional energy was better spent focused on what we needed to do to help our daughter. He explained that Faith's condition was nothing life-threatening. He had arranged an appointment with the Cleft Clinic at the Children's Hospital of Pittsburgh for Monday morning. He did his best to reassure us that Faith would be fine. However, as you can imagine, his words fell on skeptical ears. Our confidence in him and the hospital had been shaken like the walls of a house would be shaken by a tremor. But our faith in God was the solid foundation that kept the house from crashing down. When the room emptied and it was just Angie, Faith and me preparing to go home for a long weekend, I held Angie's hand with a firm grip. I began to pray. "Lord, we do not know what to think or what to feel. We do not know what lies ahead, but by faith we are trusting in You to help us. Please bring us the right doctors and help us bring You glory through this. Amen."

This was not how we expected this day to unfold, but expecting life to turn out exactly as you plan is unrealistic. Trusting in the sovereign hand of God does not mean we should not plan for or hope for life to be as we would have it. It simply means we have faith in God's love, wisdom and strength when life does not go according to our plan, trusting that His plan for our lives is what is best. This was not how we expected this day to turn out, but it was exactly how God knew it would unfold. He knew every detail of Faith's birth before she took her first labored breath. Looking back, I can see how we prepared for the birth of our daughter Faith, but God had prepared our hearts for a new level of faith that came to life that day.

DISCUSSION QUESTIONS
Chapter 2

1. Circle the things you believe would cause you to be anxious or worried.

   A strained relationship   Spilled milk
   An unexpected bill   The future
   An important interview   Cancer
   A wrench thrown into your busy schedule   A big test

2. Read Matthew 6:25-34. Jesus commanded us to live a worry-free life. Do you believe a worry-free life is possible? (Not a *problem*-free life, a *worry*-free life.) Why or why not?

   Most Christians believe God is loving. Most Christians believe God is powerful. Why do so many Christians view a worry-free life as such a challenge? What would it take for you to live your life this way?

3. Jesus makes a statement in Matthew 6:25 that seems contradictory at first glance. He asserts that "life is more important than food" and the "body is more important than clothes." Yet without food we have no life and without clothes our bodies are exposed. The point Jesus is making is clarified for us in verses 26, 28-30. What is that point?

4. Read verse 27 again. Make a list of all the benefits of worrying. Contrast this list with a list of all the things worrying can NOT do.

Benefits of Worry	Things Worry Cannot Do
_____	_____
_____	_____
_____	_____
_____	_____
_____	_____
_____	_____
_____	_____
_____	_____

Why Do We Worry?

5. Read verse 33. The fact that Jesus replaces the emphasis of our daily concerns for food, water and clothing with a concentration on God's kingdom and righteousness tells us WHAT about how Jesus sees life? Is this how you tend to see life? Why or why not?

6. Between WORRY and APATHY is where FAITH lives. How do we know we are living a life of faith and not just one of apathy (disconnected or shut off from feelings and emotions)?

    Do you tend naturally to lean more toward worry or apathy? How do we avoid these two extremes and live a life of faith?

Chasing After Faith

Life rarely turns out the way we plan. "Trusting God does not mean we should not plan for or hope for life to be as we would have it. It simply means we have faith in God's love, wisdom and strength when life does not go according to our plan."

Use the space below to describe one or two things that did not go as you hoped this week. Write about how you reacted to these unexpected moments. Then pray and ask God to give you faith in His love, wisdom and strength.

_____

_____

_____

_____

_____

_____

_____

_____

_____

_____

_____

_____

_____

_____

_____

_____

_____

Chapter 3
Giving Thanks for Faith

"Do not be anxious about anything, but in everything, by prayer and petition, with thanksgiving, present your requests to God. [7]
And the peace of God, which transcends all understanding, will guard your hearts and your minds in Christ Jesus."
Philippians 4:6-7 (NIV)

Monday morning seemed more like two weeks away rather than two days. So when the cold fall morning finally arrived we made the two-hour trip through a light snowfall to the Children's Hospital. We were not familiar with the hospital, or the city for that matter, so we felt clueless trying to find the Cleft Clinic. We arrived at the hospital and navigated our way through the colorful hallways with bewildered looks and apprehensive hearts. It may seem silly, but I felt a great sense of accomplishment when we finally found the office, so I looked at Angie and with bravado in my voice said, "I'm like Indiana Jones!" Angie seemed more focused on our appointment than impressed with my explorer instincts. As we sat in the small, boxy waiting room, my eyes scanned the walls; they were decorated with pictures of children that have benefited from the specialized surgical hands of the doctors. After a short wait, a nurse emerged and called for Faith Lingenfelter. We were escorted into a small, colorful, two-chair exam room, adorned with medical charts featuring the oral anatomy of small children. A typical examination table lined one of the walls, and a cute little toy box containing some toddler toys and a plentiful supply of children's books was tucked into the corner. We sat quiet, our calm veneer hiding our nervous hearts. At one point I looked over at Angie and made a distorted face and grunted softly in an attempt to lighten the tension. Angie glared back like she was not amused, but I could tell she appreciated the effort.

Finally a nurse entered the room, clipboard in hand, and with a kind demeanor introduced herself. Her initial examination was friendly and casual until the pulse oximeter she attached to Faith's toe showed a low level of oxygen in her blood. The nurse remained calm and professional but the concern on her face was obvious. She tried another meter in hopes that the original meter may have been faulty, but the second meter revealed an equally low amount of oxygen in her blood. Within a matter of minutes our brief consultation about a cleft surgery (a year away) turned into a more immediate need to treat pneumonia (a result of aspirating fluid into her lungs after birth). We did not waste time getting angry at those whose negligence caused this condition. Instead, our emotional energy was better spent being thankful for the competent hands now surrounding us. So many times in life we come to forks in the road. It is a divergence of perspectives that leads either to positive or negative thinking.

The apostle Paul wrote a letter to the Philippian believers while he was in prison. His incarceration was not due to wild living or depraved behavior, but rather for spreading the gospel of Jesus Christ. Paul found himself facing not only jail time, but a choice in perspective. He could have pitied himself or been angry with God about his circumstances. Instead Paul chose to be THANKFUL for the believers in Philippi who had sent him aid while he was in prison. In Philippians 4:4 Paul writes, "*Rejoice! I will say it again, rejoice!*" Then in verse 8 Paul instructs the reader to avoid sour attitudes, resentment and self-pity by meditating on, choosing to refocus our thoughts on, things that are "true, honorable, right, pure, lovely, admirable, excellent and worthy of praise."

The unpleasant truth about us is that we have a natural bent toward the negative. The reason Paul challenges us to DWELL on positive things is because we naturally dwell on the negative. We tend to think about our problems. We dwell on our disappointments and shortcomings. We replay our hurts over and over again in our minds. We measure ourselves in terms of what we cannot do rather than rejoicing in what we can do. We measure others in terms of their shortcomings rather than their good qualities. We evaluate our circumstances based on whether or not they are pleasant or comfortable rather than focusing on the spiritual significance this season of life may bring into our lives. When we come to these "crossroad" moments in life, we rarely have a choice in how circumstances turn out. The choice we have to make is one of perspective, attitude, and thinking. The very fact that Paul commands us twice to "rejoice" despite our circumstances reminds us that our thinking is our choice. We may like to blame our thinking on others or our circumstances, but it is our choice. If we wait for all to be right in the world before we have a better attitude we are going to be miserable most of our lives.

It was with great compassion in his voice the doctor explained why we would not be going home that day. Within an hour after arriving in Pittsburgh we found ourselves in a hospital room standing beside our tiny girl as a nurse fitted her with an IV and oxygen mask. She looked so frail and helpless – a reflection of our emotional state. Social services helped us get a room for the night in a hotel within walking distance of the hospital, although I think we did more praying than sleeping that first night. We were not at all prepared to spend the week in Pittsburgh, so my dad and sister, Michelle, came Tuesday night with clean clothes and lots of love from home. It is amazing how a tight hug and clean underwear can boost your spirits. Their presence and encouragement was like seeing the lead flag of the cavalry rise up over the hill, while we were pinned down and outmanned in the valley during an epic battle with fear. Knowing that the "flag" represented the prayer warriors riding into battle on our behalf brought a great sense of relief.

At the beginning of the week we had fully expected to be home for Thanksgiving dinner, but instead Angie and I gave thanks in the hospital cafeteria. Though it may be hard to believe, we truly did have much to be thankful for that day. God had blessed us with a beautiful baby girl and the best medical care in our region to help care for her. God had blessed us with family who cared for our other two children while we were two hours away and who had traveled four hours just to bring us clean clothes and uphold us in prayer. And God had given us a calm assurance that He is always in control.

Ironically, this attitude of thankfulness is something we had learned in Thanksgivings past. Thanksgiving Day was very important to my mom. It was the one time of year we got out the crystal glasses, good china dishes and fancy silverware. Our extended family, some 20 people, would gather around the three-leaf pine table for a feast of epic proportions. The turkey may have been the traditional headliner for the day, but my mom's sweet potato casserole and baked apples seemed to steal the show. We first found out my mom had cancer two days after Thanksgiving and she was taken into emergency surgery that Monday. Thanks to a talented surgeon and the Lord's mighty hand she pulled through the surgery and endured the chemotherapy that followed. As the family gathered for Thanksgiving the following year our hearts were filled with a deeper gratitude to have each other around that table than in years past. And to have a cancer survivor among us was an irrefutable reminder of how precious and fragile life really is.

Three years later Mom missed Thanksgiving when her cancer came back and she needed to have another serious surgery. Ten years after her original diagnosis my mom passed away just weeks before Thanksgiving. Thanksgiving was a day that my mom used to express her love and thankfulness for family, so not to have her at the center of it for the last couple years had seemed like traveling hours to see Niagara Falls only to find the water had been diverted and the falls were dry. It's still technically Niagara Falls, but not at all the same without the water. Another life lesson: tender turkey, perfectly browned marshmallows over sweet baked apples, and fine dinnerware are not what really matters in life. Our relationships are what truly matter on a day set aside to give thanks.

So as Angie and I held hands and bowed our heads in the crowded and noisy cafeteria, we offered God our thankful hearts. Far too often we let the vicissitudes of life rob us of joy when simple hearts of thankfulness would preserve peace in our souls. The apostle Paul put it this way when writing to the Christians in Philippi, *"Do not be anxious about anything, but in everything, by prayer and petition, with thanksgiving present your requests to God. And the peace of God, which transcends all understanding, will guard your hearts and your minds in Christ Jesus"* (Philippians 4:6-7, NIV).

DISCUSSION QUESTIONS
Chapter 3

1. Mark wrote about the moment his sister and dad arrived in Pittsburgh. *"Their presence and encouragement was like seeing the lead flag of the cavalry rise up over the hill, while we were pinned down and outmanned in the valley during an epic battle with fear. Knowing that the 'flag' represented the prayer warriors riding into battle on our behalf brought a great sense of relief."*

    Give an example of a time when you experienced the comfort and encouragement of others. Was it a moment you were thankful for? Was it a moment you could rejoice in? Why or why not?

2. As Paul sat in a Roman prison he wrote something challenging about our life perspective. Read Philippians 4:4-8.

    What did Paul have to "rejoice" about?

    How do prayer and thanksgiving overcome anxiety, fear and worry?

    What keeps us from praying and having a thankful attitude in life?

3. Philippians 4:8. Write each of the qualities we ought to be thinking about in the circles to the right. Make a list of the opposites of each quality inside the collection of circles.

    We have a natural bent toward the negative thinking represented in the center of these circles. But negative thoughts, left to ferment in our minds, tend to turn sour and then eventually poison our perspective, behavior, words and attitudes. The things in the

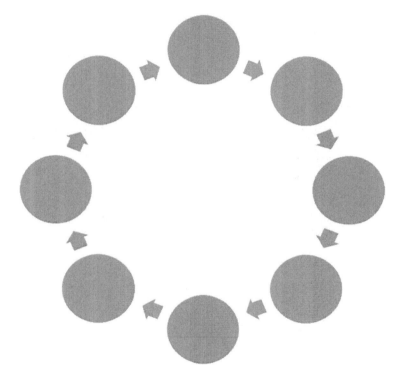

middle that we tend to make the focus of our thoughts need to be expelled from our thinking (cross out those negative words). We must then make a conscious choice to set our focus on the things represented in the shaded circles. Give an example of something you are having a struggle rejoicing over right now. Identify **ONE** thing about or in spite of your circumstance that you can be thankful for. Write it out.

Chasing After Faith

Write a "Thank You" card to Jesus. Be specific about everything you have to be thankful for. Be sure to consider the difficult circumstances or challenges in your life right now. Ask Jesus to help you see the blessings and reasons to rejoice. Be sure to thank Him for not abandoning you when you need Him the most.

Chapter 4
Almost Losing Faith

"If you had faith even as small as a mustard seed,
you could say to this mulberry tree, 'May you be uprooted
and thrown into the sea,' and it would obey you!"
Luke 17:6 (NLT)

The day after Thanksgiving, Faith was discharged. We brought her home with an oxygen backpack and orders to return the following Monday for a follow-up appointment. Very few parents get a full night's sleep when they bring a new child into their home, but these two nights at home were not broken up by the familiar sound of crying; rather, they were broken up by the heart-racing siren of an oxygen alarm that kept us not only awake but on edge.

We returned to Pittsburgh Monday morning with even more consternation than our first trip a week before. I suppose we both hoped our visit with Dr. Decker would result in a pneumonia-free report, but based on the number of times the oxygen sensor had gone off the past two days, we suspected this would not be the outcome. When Dr. Decker asked us to sit down with him, our concerns were confirmed. With genuine love in his voice he said, "Sorry guys, but Faith is going to have to stay a few days." Sad, but not surprised, we accepted the circumstances with confidence in God's will, but were unaware of the measure of faith it would require to continue trusting God's sovereign plan.

Over the next several days Dr. Decker proved to be the man God chose to use to accomplish His work that was being revealed to us one unpleasant experience at a time. Dr. Decker had ordered a number of tests, suspecting other developmental defects. The ophthalmologist discovered underdevelopment in her eyes. The urologist discovered a pelvic kidney and a malformed urethra. The cardiologist discovered a hole between the upper two chambers of her heart. One by one the specialists marched into our room revealing another layer of deficiency and stripping away another layer of our courage to hear it. At one point Angie looked at me with frazzled eyes and said, "If one more doctor comes in here with a bad report, I'm going to lose it. Enough! This is enough!"

And then it happened. Faith's oxygen levels bottomed out. The alarms went off. She turned blue and within seconds the room filled with doctors and nurses doing their best to keep Faith with us. The moment I realized Faith's oxygen had dropped through the floor, so did my heart. Then my heart bounced and lodged itself in my throat making me feel like I might throw up. Wanting to save my daughter's life and rescue my wife from the end of the rope she was dangling from, but inadequate to do either, I gathered Angie in my arms, held her tightly and began to pray. It was more of a reflex than a conscious choice over any number of inappropriate responses. Looking back, I can see how my mother's commitment to training me in prayer and a strong belief in the sovereignty of God resulted in creating this kind of "calm in the storm" moment for me.

What do you pray for in a moment like this? Perhaps some would try to bargain with God. I knew I had nothing to barter with. Perhaps some would try to manipulate God with one of those, "If you do this for me, I'll do this for you" kind of prayers. I knew God wasn't interested in such a juvenile attempt at bribery. So I just prayed for God's help! I asked Him to help Faith; to help the doctors; to help the nurses…I asked him to help us. "Help us accept Your will in whatever happens. Help us remember that this little girl belongs to You. Help us be a good testimony if you choose to take Faith to heaven. Help us to stay strong in our marriage even if we experience such a tremendous loss. We need your HELP!"

As Faith's oxygen levels began to return to normal, the room seemed to stop spinning. I'm not sure how long it was until our pale faces returned to normal, but we felt obvious relief as the room began to empty of doctors. One by one they dismissed themselves, each making eye contact with us, providing reassurance and the opportunity for us to say, "thank you." Then in a quiet moment, Angie and I gave thanks to God for His grace and mercy. We thanked Him for rescuing our daughter and for using the doctors to do so. We gave thanks for the trials we had experienced and the strength to endure them. We offered God thanks when we took our precious baby home two weeks later, and we prayed with thanksgiving over every challenge that followed. We didn't think we could handle one more moment of discouragement, but as we were sinking into the pits of despair, God's arm was not too short to reach us and pull us up no matter where the bottom of the pit ended. *"Surely the arm of the LORD is not too short to save, nor his ear too dull to hear"* (Isaiah 59:1, NIV).

These are the moments in life that challenge our faith, moments of crisis that stretch us and test our pliability. Why do some people break while others seem to bend in an extension of faith? Are some born with more intestinal fortitude than others? Are we blessed to be strong or doomed to be weak solely on the basis of the example our parents modeled before us? Certainly our personality and the emotional, spiritual and psychological patterns of our parents play a key role in how we view our circumstances and the world around us. There is no denying that I have an innate calm demeanor and I am very thankful for parents who modeled faith in the face of trials. However, I do not believe the absence of these gifts means we are destined to live a life of fear or despair. Romans 8:15 says, *" This resurrection life you received from God is not a timid, grave-tending life. It's adventurously expectant, greeting God with a childlike 'What's next, Papa?'"* (MSG)

So what then is the secret to facing our troubles and trials with the elasticity of faith and thanksgiving? The apostle Paul spoke about his trials this way, *"But we have this treasure in earthen vessels, so that the surpassing greatness of the power will be of God and not from ourselves; we are afflicted in every way, but not crushed; perplexed, but not despairing;*

persecuted, but not forsaken; struck down, but not destroyed" (2 Corinthians 4:7-9, NASB). A treasure is often something of great value hidden from plain sight, and in this case the treasure many people fail to see is the "power of God" at work. Isaiah 43:1-3 says this about God's help in times of trouble: "*But now, this is what the LORD says… 'Do not fear, for I have redeemed you; I have summoned you by name; you are mine. When you pass through the waters, I will be with you; and when you pass through the rivers, they will not sweep over you. When you walk through the fire, you will not be burned; the flames will not set you ablaze. For I am the LORD, your God, the Holy One of Israel, your Savior…'*" (NIV).

God is the source of spiritual and emotional strength that we need in life, but how do we access the power grid? The simple answer is "through faith and prayer." However, for some people that is like saying "climb" when they ask "How do I get to the top of Mount Everest?" "Climb" is indeed the simple and correct answer, but not quite sufficient for the novice mountain climber. When Angie and I thought we might lose our daughter it was indeed "faith and prayer" that kept us from losing our "FAITH," but the meaning of those words for us is rooted in knowledge and understanding of God's Word.

We believe that God is sovereign because the Bible teaches God is sovereign. "*Sovereign LORD, my strong deliverer, you shield my head in the day of battle*" (Psalm 140:7 NIV).

We believe God has a good plan for our lives because the Bible teaches this about God. *"'For I know the plans I have for you,' declares the LORD, 'plans to prosper you and not to harm you, plans to give you hope and a future'*" (Jeremiah 29:11, NIV).

We believe that God answers our prayers according to His good plan for our lives because that is what the Bible reveals to us about God. *"In the same way, the Spirit helps us in our weakness. We do not know what we ought to pray for, but the Spirit himself intercedes for us with groans that words cannot express. And he who searches our hearts knows the mind of the Spirit, because the Spirit intercedes for the saints in accordance with God's will. And we know that in all things God works for the good of those who love him, who have been called according to his purpose*" (Romans 8:26-28, NIV).

Questions like "Why isn't God listening to my prayers?" or "If God is going to do whatever He wants anyway, then why bother praying?" are rooted in a shallow understanding of the nature and character of God and a misapplication of the promises He has made in His Word. Statements like "I don't understand why God is doing this to my daughter. She never did anything wrong." reveal a misunderstanding of the nature of sin and the consequences of living in a world broken by sin. This is why the study of God's Word, both with other Christians and in one's own personal time, is so essential for the life of the Christian. When you go to a Bible study or sit down in your quiet place to read God's Word, you are not just performing some empty religious activity. You are preparing your heart and mind for battle. You are training for taking on the troubles and trials that will inevitably come to us all.

Most Christians are familiar with these words of Jesus: "*If you had faith even as small as a mustard seed, you could say to this mulberry tree, 'May you be uprooted and thrown into the sea,' and it would obey you!*" (Luke 17:6-8, NLT). Yet so many Christians seem to waffle and waver in the winds of life as if they could not muster up enough "faith" to convince God to do what they want. Lack of "FAITH" is not the problem. Lack of understanding God's Word is the problem. It takes very little amounts of faith to ask God for big things, but the more we understand who God is and why He wants us to pray in the first place, the more steadfast and anchored we become in our faith. So when you find yourself "losing faith," don't look for some magical formula to pray or reach for some good luck charm to rub – reach for and search your BIBLE! It contains the hidden treasure you seek to keep you from losing one ounce of FAITH!

DISCUSSION QUESTIONS
Chapter 4

1. Describe a time in your life when you experienced some form of doubt. Perhaps it was a moment when your faith got a little wobbly. How did you resolve this crisis of faith? What conclusions did you come to and on what did you base these conclusions?

2. At the end of this chapter Mark challenges the reader to search the Bible for the hidden treasure we need to keep us from "*losing our faith*." Take some time to read the following Scripture passages. What does each verse reveal about God? What does each verse teach us about how we ought to view our circumstances in life?

    Isaiah 43:1-3; 59:1

    Romans 8:15, 26-28

    2 Corinthians 4:7-9

    Psalm 140:7

    Jeremiah 29:11

    Luke 17:6-8

3. In Matthew 22:23-28 the Sadducees tried to stump Jesus with what they thought to be an impossible riddle. Read their supposed theological quandary then read Jesus' response in verses 29-30.

    Where did they make their error?

    How do many people today make errors in their judgment, conclusions, and perspective because of a lack of knowledge or understanding of God's Word?

What is the solution to a lack of knowledge and understanding of God's Word?

4. Read the following verses...

5. Why is Scripture useful to us? In what ways is Scripture useful for dealing with our challenges in life? Use the space around the gears to write your response.

Chasing After Faith

Identify the most recent challenge you have faced. Think of something that has stretched your faith or even caused you to question God's goodness. Use whatever tools you have available to you to search God's Word for promises or principles that apply to your situation.

For example: "I lost my job. I'm wondering how this could be for my good. I'm questioning whether or not God still cares. So I search God's Word and find comfort and courage in passages like Matthew 6:25-34, Romans 8:26-28 and Jeremiah 29:11."

(If you don't have any good Bible helps, feel free to use the verses from this chapter. Also consider saving money to buy a good study or topical Bible.)

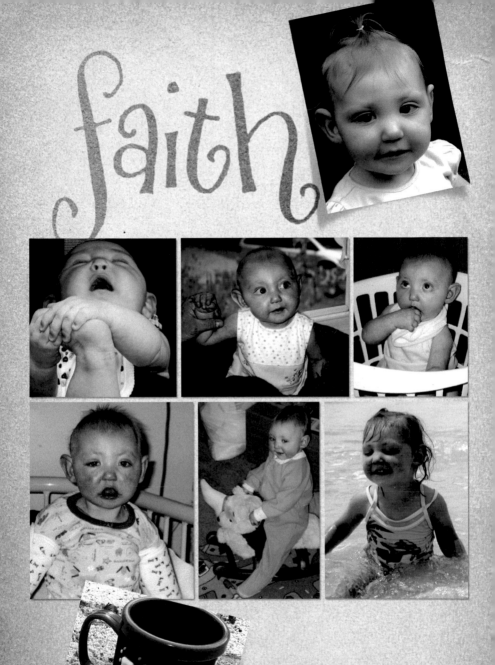

faith

The Early Years

Faith at Play

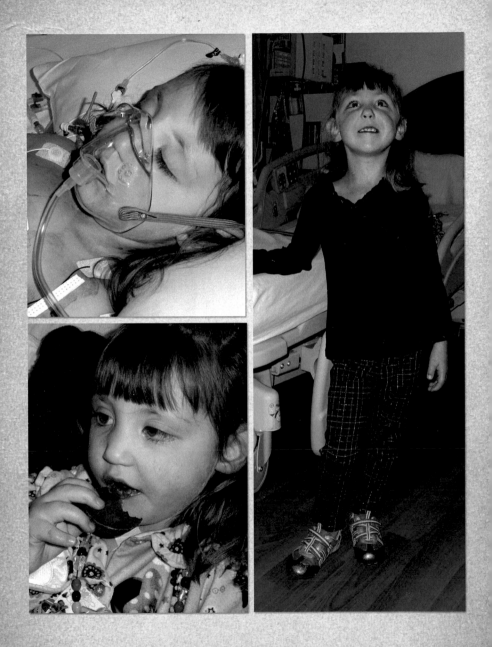

Hospital

Family

Chapter 5

Learning to Live with Faith

*"Consider it pure joy, my brothers, whenever you face
trials of many kinds, because you know that
the testing of your faith develops perseverance."*
James 1:2-3 (NIV)

Although I could write a five-part novel based on Faith's medical folders, I would rather take you on a fast-forward journey through her first four years so I can introduce you to the amazing little person Faith is becoming. She had her first cleft repair surgery when she was one and another when she was three. In between Faith received lots of in-home therapy for speech, eating, and motor skills. She has been about a year to two years behind in almost every category of development, but we have seen steady progress; and like most parents who yearn to teach their children to walk and talk, once she began we started to wonder if teaching these skills was really the best decision. From the time she leaps out of bed and bounces out her bedroom door in the morning, Faith does not stop moving or talking until her exhausted little body collapses onto her bed that night.

Between ages two and three it seemed like Faith's goal for the day was to be wherever she was not supposed to be and touch whatever was off-limits. I know that almost every child has this adventuresome spirit, but for Faith there seemed to be a total disconnect between the discipline we provided or the possible danger of her actions and her unquenchable desire to explore and live outside the boundaries. If there was a door in the room, Faith wanted to be on the other side of it. If there was a fan running, you could count on her to try to stick her fingers in the blades. And even after we corrected her and explained the danger of her actions in explicit terms, five minutes later she would try to sever her fingers again. When walking in a parking lot we literally cannot let go of her hand for a second or she will immediately run in whatever direction she is facing, like a dog that you cannot trust off the leash lest she run amok through the neighborhood. Faith requires physical tethering of some type at all times when outside the home. I used to think that parents who strap those backpack leashes to their child to keep track of them were lazy and incompetent...now I get it.

But as exhausting and frustrating as Faith can be, her sense of humor and lack of social restraint make her one of the most adorable children I have ever had the pleasure to know. On one of our annual trips to the beach, on the very same boardwalk where we chose her name, Angie and Faith were leaving the bathroom when Faith reached up, patted a very large bathroom attendant on her rotund belly and said with great enthusiasm, "See ya later!" The next day, while standing in line to use the same bathroom, Faith reached up and smacked a young girl wearing a bikini on the butt, and with a very friendly voice said, "Hi lady!" While strolling through a Disney store we found a pair of pink Minnie Mouse shoes with Minnie's face staring up from the toes. When Faith saw them she exclaimed, "Hallelujah, Hallelujah!" Moments later she was inviting a complete stranger to her birthday party (six months ahead of time). One ordinary Monday, we were doing our weekly grocery shopping. With list in hand, Angie collected the weekly provisions. I pushed the cart and Faith greeted each passing customer from her grocery cart containment seat (emphasis on the word containment). As we passed by an overweight woman, in the snack aisle of all places, Faith greeted the woman with a smile and in her sweet voice said, "Hi! Are you having a baby?" The woman looked at me. I looked at the woman. Neither of us knew what to say. So, I did the only noble thing a man could do in a situation like this. I put my head down and strolled away as quickly as possible.

My daughter Faith is both my greatest joy and my greatest frustration within moments of each other. Having Faith in my life has taught me to be more patient (a weakness God knew needed strengthened). I have learned to see the beauty of special-needs children. In the "pre-Faith" years I used to look at parents caring for special-needs children and quietly pray, "Lord, thank you for blessing us with 'normal' children," as if the parents of these children had been burdened with some unbearable affliction (or as if my other two children are the definition of "normal"). But now I realize what every parent of a special-needs child knows – these children are amazing just the way they are. God made them with a purpose and a special beauty that touches your very soul in the same way the irregular, asymmetrical shape of the bonsai tree lifts your spirits because of its imperfections. I have discovered an entirely new level of love that I did not know I was capable of. And so I give thanks for the challenges of living with my little Faith!

I believe this is the perspective God would desire us to have toward the suffering we experience in this life. The apostle Paul wrote, "*...we rejoice in our suffering, because we know that suffering produces perseverance, perseverance, character, and character, hope. And hope does not disappoint us, because God has poured out his love into our hearts by the Holy Spirit whom he has given us*" (Romans 5:2b-5, NIV).

Suffering takes a myriad of shapes and sizes. Sometimes suffering comes in the form of physical problems. Sometimes persecution will be the suffering we are forced to bear. There will be days when suffering looks more like a car in need of repair or a bill that needs paid. On other days suffering will mean we have lost a job or a loved one. Although the size and shape of suffering may vary, it is the testing of our faith that develops the underrated character quality of perseverance.

James put it this way: "*Consider it pure joy, my brothers, whenever you face trials of many kinds, because you know that the testing of your faith develops perseverance. Perseverance must finish its work so that you may be mature and complete, not lacking anything*" (James 1:2-4, NIV).

I don't know too many people who make it their goal in life to be immature and incomplete. They may be so, but not because they have charted a course to arrive in such an underdeveloped condition.

I don't know too many parents who desire to set their children loose into the world with no understanding of what it means to persevere. Yet, without the trials of a lousy coach or a difficult class we would never learn to stick it out when things get tough. Without the failure on the test or the loss of the game we would never learn a humble and gracious spirit. Without the pain of a friend that abandons us we would never understand the HOPE of a better day coming. Without the suffering of sickness and death we don't learn to trust God with our whole selves.

Perseverance is a character quality that only grows out of the soil of suffering. It cannot be learned in the absence of trouble. It is no challenge to stick it out when something is enjoyable. We do not ENDURE a pleasurable massage. We ENJOY it. Perseverance is the ability to patiently endure and the strength to not give up when challenges come. Perseverance is a character quality that allows us to experience spiritual joy. Spiritual joy is not to be confused with happiness. Happiness is contingent on circumstances and emotions. Spiritual joy, however, is a positive perspective that transcends our circumstances and emotions. Perseverance is the key that unlocks the door to spiritual joy.

Having a daughter with special needs has taught me what it means to "rejoice" in suffering and embrace the JOY that is connected with life's many trials. Without difficulties, trials, setbacks, disappointments and hardship we would never develop the character qualities we need to become stronger and more mature. It is the difficulties of life that teach us we can depend on God. It is the trials of life that teach us to run to God for shelter and courage in the storm and teach us to stay close to Him and enjoy His company when the sun shines. It is in suffering that we learn how to live a life of FAITH!

DISCUSSION QUESTIONS
Chapter 5

1. Have your children ever done or said anything to embarrass you? Consider sharing one of these experiences.

   If you can relate to Mark's description of parenting as being both his *"greatest joy and greatest frustration within moments of each other"* – explain why.

2. Read Romans 5:2-5. We tend to put the brakes on this passage as soon as we get to the "rejoice in suffering" part. These two words seem incompatible. We often think that misery ought to accompany suffering. Why does Paul say rejoicing ought to accompany suffering?

3. Read James 1:2-4. Have you ever considered the possibility that a lack of joy during life's trials may reveal immaturity in our lives? Based on these verses can you explain the connection?

4. What do the following passages teach us about PERSEVER-ANCE?

   2 Thessalonians 2:15-17

   2 Timothy 2:1-3

   Titus 1:9

   Ephesians 6:13

5. Describe a time in your life when you needed to persevere. Where did you find the strength to stick it out? Or, why did you give up?

    What does it take to be a person who perseveres?

6. Read 2 Peter 1:5-9. Fill in the boxes with qualities we are to add to FAITH.

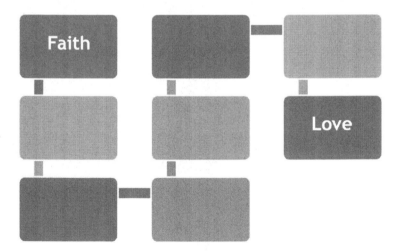

What does this passage teach us about perseverance? What do we learn about the connection between FAITH and LOVE? What do we learn about the connection between these qualities and living an effective and productive Christian life?

Chasing After Faith

Think about the difficulties trials, setbacks, disappointments, and hardships that you have experienced in life. Have you given God room to use the experience to help you grow and become stronger? Have you allowed the Holy Spirit to teach you the skills of perseverance and endurance?

Get somewhere alone so that you can be completely honest with yourself. Write down the last five challenges you have faced. Did you quit or stick it out? Did you learn any life lessons or were you too busy pouting? What did this challenge reveal about your character?

Take some time to be alone with God and talk to Him about these experiences. Ask Him to make you stronger in your faith. Ask Him to give you the ability to persevere when the next challenge in your life comes.

Chapter 6
The Heart of Faith

*"The fundamental fact of existence is that this trust in God,
this faith, is the firm foundation under everything that makes
life worth living. It's our handle on what we can't see."*
Hebrews 11:1 (MSG)

What do you do when things don't turn out the way you want? When your prayers aren't answered in the way you asked? Then what? Do you pout or throw yourself a pity party? Do you get angry and lash out at others or at God? Do you crumble under the crushing weight of anxiety? Maybe you begin to question God's love or attention. Perhaps you allow the weeds of bitterness, disappointment or cynicism to choke out the roses of joy before they have a chance to bloom. If you ever find yourself headed down paths of negative thinking, just stop where you are, sit down, and reevaluate your circumstances from a perspective of FAITH.

The Bible says that *"Faith is being SURE of what we hope for and CERTAIN of what we do not see"* (Hebrews 11:1, TNIV; capitalization added for emphasis). This is the HEART of FAITH! Faith is not about wishing on a star or crossing your fingers hoping everything will turn out the way you want. Faith believes that God is in control even when life does not take the path we would have chosen. Faith trusts God to do what is best. Faith allows God to define what is "best." Faith puts our hearts and minds at rest during the storm because we believe God can calm the storm or see us through it. Faith is a confident assurance that even if the worst (from our perspective) happens, God has not abandoned us or forgotten about us. Rather, God is right there with us in our sorrow and despair to offer comfort and strength.

There was a man named Joseph who had been betrayed by just about everyone in his life. His brothers sold him into slavery. Joseph's slave owner's wife tried to seduce him; when he refused her advances she lied to her husband and Joseph found himself in prison for a rape he did not commit. When one of Joseph's prison friends was released from prison he promised Joseph he would not forget about him, but that promise was broken. You might think that after all this betrayal in Joseph's life he would be angry and bitter toward God and all the people in his life who had hurt him. Yet everything that Joseph had been through had prepared him to rescue the nations of his day from starvation. His brothers' act of jealous hatred led him to Potipher's house. Potipher's wife's deceit landed him in the Egyptian prison where he gained a reputation for the God-given ability to interpret dreams. Joseph's rise from slave to Pharaoh's second-in-command was not an accident. As odd as it may seem, Joseph's prison experience was the path God used to lead him to the seat of power that saved the nations from a seven-year drought.

In an epic twist of irony Joseph's brothers had to come to Egypt to get food, and the man holding the keys to the pantry was the brother they had written off as dead. Yet when Joseph had the opportunity for revenge the words that came out of his mouth in that moment were words of grace and mercy toward his brothers. Joseph did not use words of anger or bitterness, but rather words of FAITH in God's sovereign hand. He said, *"You intended to harm me with your actions, but God intended it for GOOD to accomplish what is now being done, the saving of many lives"* (Genesis 50:20, NIV- capitalization added for emphasis). This is a picture of a heart full of FAITH! Each one of those betrayals hurt, but Joseph's faith in God's plan for his life protected his heart from bitterness.

In the weeks leading up to Faith's open heart surgery we spent much time in prayer. A multitude of faithful prayer warriors joined us in petitioning God on behalf of our daughter. To be honest, Angie and I did not pray for a miraculous healing. We believed God could have provided such a miracle, but we chose to pray for God's will. And if surgery was His will for Faith's life then we simply asked God to provide the right surgeon and provide healing through the hands He had equipped to do so.

There are lots of places that Angie and I could have been born. There are lots of places that we could have accepted jobs and lived. Yet this was the path that God provided. This was the path that led us to Dr. Decker, Dr. Losee (the cleft palate surgeon), and now to Dr. Morelle (the heart surgeon). As we met with Dr. Morelle during Faith's pre-op visit he described the procedure he was going to perform. He would cut through the skin, the sternum, and the pericardium to get to Faith's heart. He and his team would temporarily stop her heart, repair the hole and shock the heart back into rhythm. As he described the procedure I confess I was a little unnerved by the thought of opening up my daughter's chest and intentionally stopping her heart. But before I could question the safety of this surgery, Dr. Morelle said, "I know that this sounds very difficult and overwhelming." I was thinking, "Ah, yeah! You just said you were going to stop my daughter's heart from beating! I'm certainly not UNDER-whelmed at the idea!" He continued, "But you have to understand that I've been doing this for 13 years and I've never lost anyone. The other surgeons and I do over 500 of these every year. To me this is not a difficult procedure." He did not make this statement out of arrogance or wishful thinking, but rather *confident assurance* that he was capable of handling what was to come. This confidence was rooted in his training, experience and skill. Dr. Morelle had faith in himself.

This is another picture of faith in God. Some see having faith in God's plan as something very difficult, like cutting through layers of doubt, fear and "what ifs." But although faith is a serious thing, not to be taken lightly, it really is not that difficult to believe in God's ability to handle whatever circumstance or season of life we find ourselves in. Faith in God is not wishful thinking or arrogantly thinking we can manipulate God with a special formula prayer. Rather, faith in God is a confident assurance that He is in control and His plan is best. I believe that experience plays a major role in teaching us to have such faith.

The doctor was confident because he had been through this procedure literally thousands of times. Is there anything that could possibly surprise God? Is there any challenge that is too big for His mighty hand? The answer is "no," and the reason we know this is because God has proven Himself time after time, after time, after time… James says that we should consider our trials "pure joy" because they are developing in us the character qualities of perseverance, hope and faith! It is only through the experiences of trials that we have the opportunity to believe that God's plan is good and that He will not abandon us. If these difficult situations were absent from our lives we would have no understanding of what it is like to have God hold us up when we cannot stand on our own.

If we view faith as something so difficult and complicated, like I originally viewed my daughter's heart surgery, rather than a simple act of trust, then we will continue to go through every difficult moment in life feeling like we are cutting through skin and bone to get to this mysterious unseen "faith." This perspective of faith will most likely make us feel overwhelmed by the thought and we may be unwilling to pick up the scalpel. Instead, we will worry, lose sleep, overeat or run away to avoid the real issue. Instead of choosing this path of negative thinking, STOP where you are and choose to believe God is in control. Choose to believe God's plan for your life is good. Choose to believe there is no challenge too big for God's mighty hand. Choose to believe God will always keep His promise to never abandon you. The heart of faith is not complicated or difficult to get to. The HEART of FAITH is to simply BELIEVE!

DISCUSSION QUESTIONS
Chapter 6

1. What do you do when things don't turn out the way you want? When your prayers aren't answered in the way you asked? Then what?

   Describe reactions you have seen in others or in yourself when life takes an unexpected turn toward difficult challenges.

2. Define "faith" according to Hebrews 11:1.

   _____

   _____

   _____

   What are some inadequate or incorrect definitions of "faith"?

   _____

   _____

   _____

3. In what ways do we sometimes make "faith" more complicated than it needs to be?

4. The life of Joseph is an amazing example of a man's faith in God's sovereign hand. Read the following passages in the circles below. As you reflect on the passages, answer the following questions...

If this had happened to you, what would your natural reaction have been?

What would a perspective of faith look like?

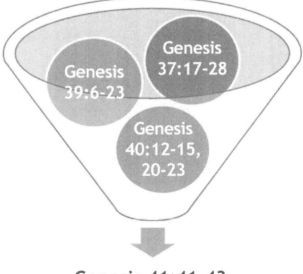

Genesis 41:41-43

5. When we get to the bottom of the funnel we find Joseph in charge. All these events led to Joseph becoming second-in-command in Egypt at the age of 30. Joseph went from the PIT, to the PRISON, to a POSITION of POWER.

Now read Genesis 42:6-7; 45:1-7; 50:20.

How was Joseph able to have such a view of his life and not hold bitter resentment toward his brothers?

A Note from the Author

"I have a close friend and ministry partner who left a previous ministry because he was wronged. He came to our ministry wounded, but God intended it all for good. He has been a tremendous blessing to my life and ministry. My greatest hurts and disappointments in ministry happened while he was by my side. Had he not been there I may have burned out. I praise God for the hurt in my friend's life because God used it to bless mine. Ironically, God used our experiences with our daughter Faith to bless my friend. Falling in love with our daughter, Faith, prepared him for dealing with the news that his own granddaughter had been born with cystic fibrosis. God intended it all for GOOD - "to accomplish what is now being done"(Genesis 50:20 - NIV) - Mark Lingenfelter

---

In what ways have you seen God's sovereign hand at work in your life? How has God used challenges in your life to bless others? How has God used the challenges that others have faced to strengthen you?

Chasing After Faith

Buy a peach or a nectarine. Wash it. Take a sharp knife and carefully cut it in half, removing the large pit inside. Look at the pit. It is hard and unattractive. It would not taste good if you tried to eat it. Now, enjoy the fruit of the peach or nectarine, but don't take your eyes off the pit. Without the PIT there would be NO fruit. The sweet fruit you are enjoying was formed around the pit. Remove the pit and you lose the fruit. Plant the pit and you give new life to another tree that will also bear good fruit.

How does the peach/nectarine illustration relate to our discussion about faith?

Chapter 7
The Miracle of Faith

MIRACLE: "God doing something supernatural
that defies the laws of the natural world."
Dr. Dave Plaster

When Doctor Morelle asked us to select a date for Faith's heart surgery we had already decided it should be the week of Thanksgiving. We came to this conclusion because God had given us so much for which to be thankful. Plus it had almost become a new family tradition to spend Thanksgiving in Pittsburgh. Although the hospital cafeteria was a far cry from the home cooked meal we would have preferred, spending four out of five years in the Steel City had become the new norm.

Angie, Faith and I spent the night before Faith's surgery at the Ronald McDonald house connected to the Children's Hospital. The accommodations were very much like a suite at a moderate quality hotel, but the atmosphere of the burdened hearts from its guests was hard to escape. Most times in life we pass by people and have no idea, nor concern, about what is happening in their lives. But in a place like this making eye contact with a stranger is like saying, "I see you. I feel what you are feeling. Hang in there." Why does this unspoken bond between souls seem to bring comfort and a sense of community? Perhaps it is reassuring to know you are not the only one who is hurting. Perhaps the suffering of others helps lift our eyes from our own circumstances long enough to see that the fallen condition of

51

the world has impacted all of us. Perhaps the emotional connection we share through suffering voids the selfishness that seeks to rob us of compassion for others. Whatever it is, I am thankful that the path of difficulty not only connects me with my fellow travelers, but with God, my traveling companion.

Before putting Faith to bed, we prayed with her and took one last picture of her chest without a scar. It was a moment of both quiet reflection and grounded uncertainty. I think we are at times tempted to look too far into the future, asking questions and setting up expectations that cannot be answered nor realistically met. But faith helps keep us in the moment. I had no control over what would take place on the operating table the next day. But I did have the opportunity to enjoy, embrace and connect with my daughter in that moment. This, I believe, is the MIRACLE of FAITH!

In seminary I learned that a "miracle" is defined as "God doing something supernatural that defies the laws of the natural world (Dr. Dave Plaster)." I know some people were praying that God would perform a miracle in Faith's body and heal her heart so she would not require surgery. And that would have been fine with us. But here we were, in Pittsburgh, preparing for open heart surgery. Does that mean that God did not provide a miracle? I believe God did provide a miracle. I believe the miracle God provided was FAITH! I believe faith itself is a gift from God. Our natural tendency is to doubt and worry; that is our default setting. But the gift of faith "defies the laws of the natural world." Faith gives us courage when fear attacks. Faith gives us hope when things look hopeless. Faith gives us a calm assurance in the storm and solid footing when the earth beneath us trembles. Faith is a gift from God that resets our default setting and reprograms our perspective. I would define that as a miracle.

Angie and I awoke early. We prepared ourselves physically, then spiritually. As we prayed together, we prayed a simple prayer of thanksgiving for all God had done to demonstrate His love and power in our lives. We asked for His will to be accomplished in Faith's life and in ours. We asked for a spirit of calmness to fill our hearts and the faith we needed to trust Him throughout the days ahead. This was Faith's fourth time under anesthesia and my fourth time to be the one to put on the attractive white paper gown, accompany her into the operating room and hold her down when it was time for the "happy" gas. I understand why they call it "happy" gas, but it never made Faith happy. Every time she sat on the table and saw the mask approach, she experienced a panic attack. She would thrash and scream until the gas forced calmness upon her little body. They tried giving her "happy" juice (some type of sedative) in the past. It only heightened her anxiety. We tried reason. We tried bribery. Yet, every time she would begin to panic from the moment they took her blood pressure till the moment she was unconscious... except for that day. That day she was CALM. No screaming, no thrashing, no crying...just calm acceptance of what needed to happen. I believe this was an answer to prayer and a miracle of faith in her life!

The surgery went as planned, and by mid-afternoon Angie and I were escorted into the cardiac ICU. As we entered the room it looked like we just stepped into a scene from a science fiction movie. Wires, tubes, flashing medical equipment and computers filled the room, and in the middle of it all was our baby girl. She was sprawled out flat on her back with a tube down her nose, another in her right arm and still another coming out of her chest just under the bandages covering her incision. It was another quiet moment of surrender. I was truly thankful the surgery went well, but it hurt to see our child hurting. Angie and I approached her bedside, unsure where to touch her. She looked so fragile. The ICU nurse assigned to Faith assured us it was OK to kiss her. We both kissed her gently on the forehead and stared in wonder at this amazing gift God had so generously given us.

Our amazement continued the next day. Faith was up and walking around the ICU unit and not even the strong pain medicine she was on could quench her personality. As we walked the halls she said "hello" to everyone who would make eye contact with her and asked a number of people for Reese's peanut butter cups. She was so pleased when one of the nurses on the floor obliged her request with a king-size pack of her favorite comfort food. It was hard to believe how quickly a child can recover from open heart surgery. Her surgery happened on a Monday and we were on our way home just three days later, once again on Thanksgiving Day! We left the hospital that day with one newly repaired heart and hundreds of very thankful hearts. We were thankful for the faithfulness of God, the excellent care of Children's Hospital and the miracle of Faith!

DISCUSSION QUESTIONS
Chapter 7

1. Just like the word "awesome," the word "miracle" gets thrown around much more than it should be. We hear people talk about the "miracle of childbirth." Giving birth to a child is a natural wonder, but it is not a miracle. The virgin conception of Jesus was a miracle. It defied the laws of the natural world. Abraham and Sarah having a child at such an old age was a miracle. It defied the laws of the natural world.

   Give some examples of amazing, wonderful life events that really should not be classified as miracles.

   Give some examples of "textbook" miracles.

Examples of Miracles in Old Testament

Creation (Gen. 1). Flood (Gen. 7-8). Fire on Abraham's sacrifice (Gen. 15:17). Destruction of Sodom (Gen. 19). Lot's wife turned to salt (Gen. 19:26). Burning bush (Ex. 3:2). Plagues in Egypt (Ex. 8-12). Passage of Red Sea (Ex. 14:22). Water from the rock (Ex. 17:5, 7). Jordan River divided (Josh. 3:14-17).

Examples of Miracles of Jesus

Turned water into wine (John 2:1-11). Catch of fish (Luke 5:1-11). Peter's mother-in-law healed (Mt. 8:14-17). Healed the paralytic (Mt. 9:1-8). Raised the widow's son to life (Luke 7:11-16). Stilled the storm (Mt. 8:23-27). Fed the 5,000 (Mt. 14:15-21). Walked on water (Mt. 14:22-33). Healed 10 lepers (Luke 17:11-19). Raised Lazarus from the dead (John 11:1-46).

---

2. Have you ever witnessed or personally experienced a miracle? (If you are a believer, you have experienced at least ONE – salvation)

   How did this miracle impact your life?

   How did faith play a role?

3. Read the following examples of miracles. What was required of those who performed the miracle or received the miracle?

   Matthew 9:27-30

   Matthew 17:14-20

   John 14:12

   Acts 3:1-16

   Acts 14:8-10

4. Why would Mark say that "FAITH" is a MIRACLE?

Chasing After Faith

God may not use you to perform physical miracles like restoring sight to the blind or mobility to the paralytic. However, God may want to perform spiritual miracles through you.

Take some time to visit a nursing home or write a card to a shut-in. Share some encouraging Scripture passages and words of HOPE with someone. The Spirit may use your kindness and love to do a miracle in someone's life. Their natural bent may be toward despair or discouragement and God may use your words of hope to change their perspective and breathe courage into their souls – resulting in a spiritual miracle. Why not give it a try?

Chapter 8
Chasing After Faith

*"His divine power has given us everything we need
for life and godliness through our knowledge of him
who called us by his own glory and goodness."*
2 Peter 1:3 (NIV)

The cardiologist told us that Faith would have more energy after the surgery to repair the hole in her heart. When he said this, Angie and I looked at each other then looked back at the doctor and said in unison, "I don't think that is possible." He assured us his diagnosis was accurate and a few short weeks of recovery proved him right! Faith is even more difficult to keep up with now. This is a blessing our family and the people at our church find it both astonishing and humorous.

Life with Faith is certainly never boring. For example, about five months after her heart surgery Faith was playing with one of her brother's mini-bungee straps and decided it would be a good idea to put it in her mouth. She somehow managed to impale the inside of her cheek with the hook. This poor decision resulted in a bloody mess followed by an impacted infection that required two days in the hospital and a minor surgery. Just another day in the unpredictable world of chasing after Faith!

I would be lying if I said there were not days that I yearn for Faith's bedtime. I would be lying if I said chasing after Faith all day is not exhausting. But when she bounces into the room dressed like a superhero-slash-princess and asks, "How do I look?" I cannot help but smile and praise God for such an amazing little girl. When she sings a song enthusiastically off-key or claps her hands in excitement over the simple things in life, I am reminded to lighten up and enjoy life. When my little Faith crawls up in my lap at the end of a non-stop day, wraps her arms around my neck and says, "I'm ready for bed now" – I am grateful for the unconditional love God has shown me and grown in me. These are the moments that make chasing after Faith worth the effort it takes to do so.

What are you chasing after in this life? Are you chasing after a more prominent career? Are you chasing after a bigger house or a nicer car? Are you chasing after popularity or some cute guy? There are a lot of things that are not worth chasing after in this life. One thing that is worth chasing after is faith. What I mean by chasing after faith is "actively pursuing a life of faith in Jesus Christ." There is so much spiritual and emotional power available to those who pursue a faith-based relationship with Jesus Christ. Unfortunately, many Christians do not live powerful lives because they do not chase after and grab hold of a life of faith. Some are too busy chasing after things that won't last. However, some just don't understand that pursuing a life of faith extends beyond the moment of salvation.

The Apostle Paul believed that faith in the power of the resurrection was the most important thing in his everyday life. In a letter to the church at Philippi he wrote, "*I want to know Christ and the power of his resurrection and the fellowship of sharing in his sufferings, becoming like him in his death*" (Philippians 3:10, NIV). Paul didn't just want to know **about** the power that raised Christ from the dead, he wanted to **experience** the power that raised Christ from the dead: not just when he died, but in this life as well!

Living a life of FAITH begins with a faith-based relationship with Jesus Christ. You must believe by faith that Jesus sacrificed His own life on the cross as a substitute payment for your sin. You must believe that Jesus rose from the dead and you must trust Jesus Christ as your forgiver of sin and savior from hell. Faith in Christ alone is the only way to spiritually prepare your soul for eternity. (For a clear and simple explanation about how YOU can begin a faith-based relationship with Jesus Christ, please see Appendix.) Every true Christian has faith in the power of the resurrection to save their soul from hell, but not every Christian has faith in the power of the resurrection for everyday life. The Apostle Peter wrote, "*His divine POWER has given us everything we need for life and godliness through our knowledge of him who called us by his own glory and goodness*" (2 Peter 1:3, NIV- capitalization added for emphasis). Do not overlook the source of this power that gives us everything we need for everyday life. It is the divine power of God. The same power that raised Jesus Christ from the dead is the power that can, and should, impact our daily lives. Faith in the power of the resurrection saves our souls, and faith in the power of the resurrection gives us what we need for everyday life. It is faith in the power of the resurrection that helps us stop living selfish lives. Just prior to Paul's declaration of his desire to experience the power of the resurrection in his life, he wrote these words,

> "*Though I could have confidence in my own effort if anyone could. Indeed, if others have reason for confidence in their own efforts, I have even more! I was circumcised when I was eight days old. I am a pure-blooded citizen of Israel and a member of the tribe of Benjamin—a real Hebrew if there ever was one! I was a member of the Pharisees, who demand the strictest obedience to the Jewish law. I was so zealous that I harshly persecuted the church. And as for righteousness, I obeyed the law without fault. I once thought these things were valuable, but now I consider them worthless because of what Christ has done. Yes, everything else is worthless when compared with the infinite value of know-ing Christ Jesus my Lord. For his sake I have discarded everything else, counting it all as garbage, so that I could gain Christ and become one with him. I no longer count on my own righteousness through obeying the law; rather, I become righteous through faith in Christ. For God's way of making us right with himself depends on faith*" (Philippians 3:4-9, NLT).

These things might not mean much to you and me, but these were the kinds of things that mattered to the people in Paul's day. In 2011 there was wall-to-wall coverage of Britain's Royal Wedding. Every major news organization got in on the action. They had fashion shows speculating what style of dress Kate might wear. They interviewed guests to review the guest list. They sent correspondents days in advance to cover this momentous day in history. I am so glad we had boots on the ground to give us hard-hitting analysis of the "first kiss." Sarcasm aside, I really do understand why Prince William is admired by so many people. He was born a prince, he has a great education, he has a great reputation as a soldier and he is wealthy and powerful. These are all things the world values. But just imagine if Prince William gathered the media together for a news conference and said, "I know all this stuff should matter to me, but it doesn't. I am not going to live as a prince. In fact, Kate and I are going to be missionaries in Africa." The news media would have a collective stroke. The headlines would read "Prince William Gone Mad."

In Paul's day, in the Jewish culture, Paul had it all. He had the right parents, the right education and the right nationality. He had wealth and power, but he considered ALL of these things rubbish (manure!). He wanted something more! Paul says he wants "to KNOW Christ." The word "know" means more than to have intellectual knowledge about Jesus. Paul uses a Greek word that means to KNOW through experience or to know personally. Paul desires a deep and intimate relationship with Jesus. Paul is saying, "I don't need all this stuff the world has to offer. Jesus is enough."

I know I am not the only one who struggles with the sin of selfishness. Things do not go the way I planned. People do not do what I want. Circumstances do not turn out the way I hoped… what happens? I get mad or upset and throw myself a pity party. Why? Selfishness! It is the subtle sin that attacks us all and unfortunately wins most of the battles it wages. Where do we find the power to stop being so selfish? Where do I find the power to think about others first? Where do I find the power to desire God's will for the day rather than plow through my own? The same power that raised Jesus from the dead is the power that will help me overcome the sin of selfishness. I must have faith in the power of the resurrection.

Not only is pursuing a life of faith the key to overcoming selfishness, but it is also the power source to endure suffering. *"I want to know Christ and the power of his resurrection and the fellowship of sharing in his sufferings, becoming like him in his death"* (Philippians 3:10, NIV). Paul says he wants to know the fellowship of sharing in the suffering of Jesus. When you first read this you might think Paul has lost it. Why would anyone want to suffer? It is not the suffering in itself that Paul desires – it is the fellowship that suffering brings. Angie and I are not the only ones who have ever had a child with disabilities. There are families who have suffered greater pains than we have. We will all experience suffering in this world. But when someone else is hurting we have an important choice to make. We can isolate ourselves from that situation so that we do not have to hurt, or we can share in (participate in; have fellowship with) the suffering and pain that the other family is experiencing.

This is what Jesus Christ did for us. He came to earth and shared in our suffering. He knows what it feels like to suffer, be rejected, lied about, accused of things He didn't do, tempted by sin, be abandoned and be betrayed. He knows what emotional and physical pain feels like. He knows what it feels like to lose someone He loved. He knows financial hardship. He KNOWS! So when we KNOW Christ through a faith-based relationship with Him, we are developing an intimate relationship with someone who has been through all the emotions and pain we experience in life. We can share our lives with Jesus. We can ask Him for comfort. We can go to Him with our struggles, fears, hurts, or suffering, and we can let Him wrap His love around us as someone who understands and cares. Jesus wants to comfort us and give us courage and strength. This is what it means to have fellowship with Jesus in His suffering. And the path to fellowship with Jesus is chasing after a life of faith.

I have met many people who tell me they blew it in life because they spent too much time working and not enough time with their children. I have seen the empty pursuit of material things that people use to make themselves feel important or valuable. I have experienced the heartache of chasing after the unrequited affections of others. On the other side of the life chasing choices is the intangible, everlasting, eternal value of pursuing a life of faith. I have never met a faithful Christian who said, "I really wasted my time serving the Lord." I have never heard a dying man or woman say, "I wish I would have spent less time in prayer and more time watching TV." A life of faith is not an emotional crutch or a waste of time. A life of faith is the key to the divine power we need for everyday life. A life of faith is what enables us to persevere and view life's challenges from a positive, thankful perspective. There are a lot of things we could chase after in this life. I have found that *CHASING AFTER FAITH* is the most valuable of them all.

DISCUSSION QUESTIONS
Chapter 8

1. What is your favorite prince/princess story?

   What is it about royalty that fascinates so many people?

   Why do the temporary things of this life seem so appealing to us?

2. Read Philippians 3:4-10.

   What did Paul have going for him from a worldly point of view?

   Why did Paul view these things as an empty pursuit?

   What did Paul desire more than money, influence, or fame?

> St. Francis of Assisi had it all. He had wealth, power, respect and influence. Yet he gave it all up to go and serve the lepers living on the outskirts of society. Why is self sacrifice an important part of faith? Why would serving others be worth pursuing?

3. Read 1 John 2:15-17. How does a desire for worldly pleasures hinder a life of faith?

4. Read 1 John 5:13-15. How does faith in God's will impact our desires and our prayer life?

5. According to the following verses, how is FAITH a powerful weapon in the battles we face in life?

   Ephesians 6:10-18

   2 Corinthians 10:2-6

   1 Thessalonians 5:8

   Hebrews 10:22-25

6. Mark mentions two reasons why pursuing a life of faith is worthwhile.

   Overcoming S_____

   Endure S_____

   Can you think of any other benefits to pursuing a life of faith?

Chasing After Faith

Write your obituary reflecting your life so far. What would you include to summarize what your life was about? Would you include your accomplishments, degrees earned, sports you played or clubs you were a member of? Would you be proud of your church membership or that you wrote a book?
How many of the things you wrote will really matter 50 years from now? How much of what your life has been about will matter in eternity?

Check your pulse. Are you still breathing? Great news! There is still time to change the story! There is still time to redefine what your life is all about. There is still time to finish strong. There is still time to chase after a life of FAITH!

What will you do to begin or continue the pursuit? Be specific!

How to Begin Your New Life in Jesus Christ Today!

Before you can become spiritually *ALIVE* you must understand that you are spiritually *DEAD*. We are all born this way. This is why we naturally chase after our own desires rather than chase after God's. When we step outside God's boundaries or beyond His limits it is called "sin" and sin is what separates us from a holy God.

> *"As it is written: 'There is no one righteous, not even one; there is no one who understands, no one who seeks God. All have turned away, they have together become worthless; there is no one who does good, not even one'"* (Romans 3:10-12, NIV).

Once we understand we have a serious spiritual problem, we are ready to accept the one true solution. Men offer a variety of opinions as to how people can be made right with God and receive eternal life in Heaven, but God only offers ONE way!

> *"God has given us eternal life and this life is in His Son {Jesus}. He who has the Son has life; he who does not have the Son of God does not have life"* (1 John 5:11-12, NIV).

> *Jesus said, "I am the way the truth and the life. No one can come to the Father except through me"* (John 14:6, NIV).

> *"Salvation is found in no one else, for there is no other name under heaven given to men by which we must be saved"* (Acts 4:12, NIV).

Beginning a spiritual relationship with God happens through simple faith in the Good News that Jesus died on the cross to pay the penalty for your sin, and belief that the resurrection of Jesus proves the price has been paid in full.

> *"For I delivered to you as of first importance what I also received, that Christ died for our sins according to the Scriptures, and that He was buried, and that He was raised on the third day according to the Scriptures" (1 Corinthians 15:3-4, NASB).*

Faith is not just about believing the FACTS of Jesus' death and resurrection. Satan and his demons know all too well that Jesus died on the cross and rose from the dead. Saving faith is when we trust with our whole selves in Jesus to keep His promise to forgive our sins and save our souls from Hell.

> *You believe that there is one God. Good! Even the demons believe that--and shudder" (James 2:19, NIV).*

> *"That if you confess with your mouth Jesus as Lord, and believe in your heart that God raised Him from the dead, you shall be saved; [10] for with the heart man believes, resulting in righteousness, and with the mouth he confesses, resulting in salvation" (Romans 10:9-10, NASB).*

> *"Say the welcoming word to God—"Jesus is my Master"—embracing, body and soul, God's work of doing in us what he did in raising Jesus from the dead. That's it. You're not "doing" anything; you're simply calling out to God, trusting him to do it for you. That's salvation. [10] With your whole being you embrace God setting things right, and then you say it, right out loud: "God has set everything right between him and me!" (Romans 10:9-10, MSG).*

God's gift of forgiveness isn't something you can earn. You have to accept it through faith in Jesus Christ alone.

> *"For it is by grace that you have been saved, through faith - this is not of yourselves, it is a gift from God - not by works, so that no one can boast." (Ephesians 2:8-9, NIV).*

When you choose to accept God's free gift of forgiveness and invite Jesus Christ to be the Leader of your life, God will not only give you eternal life after you die, but He will also give you new spiritual life now on this side of heaven. The Spirit of God will live with your spirit and begin to transform you into a new person.

"Therefore, if anyone is in Christ, he is a new creation; the old has gone, the new has come!" (2 Corinthians 5:17, NIV).

"And you also were included in Christ when you heard the word of truth, the gospel of your salvation. Having believed, you were marked in him with a seal, the promised Holy Spirit, [14] who is a deposit guaranteeing our inheritance until the redemption of those who are God's possession--to the praise of his glory" (Ephesians 1:13-14, NIV).

A Simple Prayer You Can Pray

"Dear God, I believe you love me. Please forgive me for all the wrong things I've said, thought and done. Thank you for sending Your Son, Jesus, to pay for my sins when He died on the cross. I believe Jesus rose from the dead. I trust Jesus as my Forgiver of sin and Savior from Hell. I want Him to be the Leader of my life. Please transform my life and help me live completely for YOU! Amen."

About the Author

After graduating summa cum laude from St. Francis University with a degree in sociology/pre-law, Mark E. Lingenfelter decided to change direction in life. Mark originally intended to pursue a career in sports law, but he believed God was calling him to full-time Christian ministry. Three years later, Mark graduated from Grace Theological Seminary, Winona Lake, Ind., with a Master of Arts in Ministry. He has been the lead pastor of the Leamersville Grace Brethren Church in central Pennsylvania since 2001. The "rules" say you cannot follow a pastor with a long tenure and survive. The "rules" say you cannot pastor a church that you grew up in and survive. However, God has used Mark as proof that when God calls, He equips. Not only has Pastor Mark's ministry survived, it has thrived. The church has tripled in size and continues to reach lost souls with the gospel of Jesus Christ.

Mark has been married to his high school sweetheart since 1998 and they have three children (Hannah, Elijah, Faith). Mark is not only a leader in the West Penn District of Grace Brethren churches; he is also a leader in the community as he coaches junior high football for the Spring Cove School District.

Mark's love for God and passion for the gospel have taken him to Nigeria and Thailand on short-term mission trips. He desires to present God's Word in a biblically accurate and practical way that captures the hearts and minds of those placed before him in ministry. Mark believes that *"His divine power has given us everything we need for life and godliness through our knowledge of him who called us by his own glory and goodness"* (2 Peter 1:3, NIV) and he seeks to live this truth daily.